A Handbook of
Landscape
Palms

by Jan Allyn

A Great Outdoors Book

Great Outdoors Publishing Co.
St. Petersburg, Florida

Published by:
Great Outdoors Publishing Co.
4747 28th Street North
St. Petersburg, Florida 33714
(727)525-6609
www.floridabooks.com

ISBN 0-8200-0422-X

Revised second edition 2003.

Photographs by:
Jan Allyn
Robin Cole
Roger L. Hammer
Mark Issenberg
James Phillips/Silverlake Photography

Cover photo by Jan Allyn

Printed in Canada

About Palms

Botanically, "palm trees" are more closely related to grasses and stemless plants than most of the other plants we call trees. They have their own family, named Arecaceae (or Palmae). Over two thousand species grow in the tropical and warm temperate regions of the world. Only a few, those most commonly cultivated in the United States, are described in this book. Most have been introduced to this country from Asia, Africa, Central and South America, and Australia. Among native palms, all but one species originated in Florida and the Caribbean. The exception is the Washington palm, a native of the southwestern U.S.

LEAVES. Most palms have leaves that are palmate (fan-shaped) or pinnate (feather-shaped). A very few have bipinnate leaves (having twice-divided leaflets) or entire leaves (unsegmented leaves with no leaflets). As a palm grows, it sheds its oldest, outermost leaves. In some species, like the queen palm, they are shed quite readily. In others, like the Washington palm, they may hang on for years.

TRUNKS. There are single-trunked palms, and palms that tend to sucker and form multiple trunks. Some members of the latter group produce so many suckers that they resemble huge clumps of grass, rather than trees. Trunks may be covered with spines, fiber, or nothing at all. Some palm species accumulate old leaf bases, or "boots," on the trunk. Though it does no harm to remove them, many people find the criss-cross patterns they create quite attractive and so prefer to leave them on. Some palms have a green "crownshaft" at the top of the trunk, formed by the bases of the outermost fronds. This crownshaft can be half the height of the trunk.

FLOWERS. In general, the flowers of palms are rather small, borne in clusters on a flowerstalk, and are usually white, yellow, or some color in between. As a rule, they aren't showy or fragrant. Flowers grow on stalks that emerge from among the leaves or are borne just below the crownshaft, if the palm has one. In some species the flowerstalk is protected by a boat-like spathe; the queen palm is one of these. In hermaphroditic palms, each flower has both male and female parts. In dioecious palms, male and female flowers grow on different plants. An example is the edible date palm; two trees of different sexes are required to produce fruit.

Monoecious palms have separate male and female flowers, but both grow on the same plant, either on the same or different flowerstalks.

FRUITS. Palm fruits are generally berry- or nut-like, ranging in size from the tiny, quarter inch-long fruit of the Florida thatch palm to the largest fruit on earth, the giant double coconut. These odd, edible fruits may weigh as much as forty-five pounds, and are borne by palms of the species *Lodoicea maldivica*, native to the Seychelles Islands. There are relatively few palm species that have fruit that is edible (and palatable) to people. Those described in this book are the edible date palm, the pindo palm, and the coconut. In Jonathan Dickinson's Journal, the story of a 1696 shipwreck that occurred on Florida's east coast, palm berries are described as tasting like "rotten cheese steeped in tobacco." Many species of palms have fruit that is attractive to birds and mammals, however.

Planning for a Beautiful Landscape

As a group, palms are fairly easy to grow. Most have modest water, nutritional and maintenance requirements. But before adding them—or any other plant—to your existing landscape, you would be wise to make a plan, if only in your mind.

First, take a few minutes to think about your objectives. How do you envision your landscape, your garden? What is its purpose? Will it be a place for play? Quiet contemplation? Vibrant beauty? To grow nutritious food? To provide shelter and succor for birds and other wildlife? Will it be a sunny, open space or a shady, secluded nook? How much time and effort do you want to expend on its upkeep?

Next, learn about your property. Find out what type soil it has; study the topology, microclimates, and special requirements of your "estate." This is easier than it may at first appear. Move a few shovelfuls of soil and observe whether it is sandy, clay-like, or loamy. You can have the local Cooperative Extension Service office test a soil sample to learn whether it is acid or alkaline (although for palms, this is not essential; most grow fine in either). After a heavy rain, observe where water runs off the soil and where it collects. Does water puddle and stand, or disappear into the soil? Consider the orientation of your house and its effect on light and temperature. The sides facing north and south will get the most sun; although the south-facing side is usually warmest, adjacent buildings, fences, or groves of trees may shield it from the raging summer sun. They also act as windbreaks and provide good frost protection in winter. Keep in mind that coastal areas are warmer than inland ones. Observe the location of entryways, windows, driveways and parking areas, swimming pool and heating/cooling equipment. Ensuring safe, easy access to these areas may influence your choices. Note too whether there are places where dropped fruit, flowers or leaves would pose a hazard or a nuisance. Imagine the view from inside the house—will the addition of a large plant or tree in a certain spot block or enhance it?

Once you have a picture of your ideal landscape in mind, learn about every plant before you purchase it and ask yourself whether and how it fits into your overall plan. In particular, find out how large it will get, how quickly it grows, if and when it will flower and fruit, whether it is invasive or hazardous (poisonous or spiny, for example), annual or perennial, evergreen or deciduous, and for what purposes it usually is used (hedge, groundcover, shade tree, etc.). Also learn how much water, fertilizer and light it needs, what type of soil it grows best in, and how much cold and hot weather it can take. If you live near the ocean, it is also important to know whether the plants you choose are salt tolerant.

If you do these things, you will find that you enjoy gardening more and will be more successful at it. Remember that it is essential to select plants appropriate for your climate. One thing that is beyond control in an outdoor landscape is the temperature. If an area gets too hot or too cold for a particular plant, it will not thrive—and may not survive.

Selecting the Right Palm

When choosing a palm, the most important considerations are form, size at maturity, light requirements, and cold hardiness. The form of a palm determines its landscape uses. While some cluster palms (broadleaf lady palm, areca palm, fishtail palm) may be very effective as hedges or screens, tall, single-trunked palms (Florida royal palm, edible date palm, Washington palm) are better used as street or accent plantings. Smaller single-trunked palms make lovely specimen plants in the garden, especially those with silvery or bluish-green foliage (Bismarck palm, latan palm, buccaneer palm), interesting leaves (Fiji fan palm, foxtail palm, fishtail palm) or unusual trunks (triangle palm).

Size is very important. Unlike some other plants, palms cannot be pruned to keep them small. So choose a species that will be the right size for its location when fully mature, no matter if it grows slowly or quickly. Plant tall palms that will need regular trimming (queen palm) where you can easily reach their tops. Large cluster palms (Senegal date palm, Everglades palm) should not be planted abutting walkways because as they grow they will impede foot traffic. This is especially true of Senegal date palm, whose sharp-pointed leaflets could easily cause an eye injury.

Choose the right location for your palms, keeping in mind light, frost protection and soil drainage. Palms which prefer shade may withstand full sun, but will never look their best. Their leaves may sunburn in summer or they may turn yellow. Conversely, palms that require a lot of light may survive in deep shade but grow very slowly, and they may never bloom or produce fruit. Most palms are tolerant of a wide range of soil types, provided they have good drainage. If your planting site is low or floods periodically, choose a palm like Everglades palm, dwarf palmetto, royal palm, Senegal date palm or areca palm, all of which are adapted to moister soil. Saw palmetto prefers a well-drained site but will withstand periodic flooding.

Although palms usually bring to mind images of the tropics, there are species that can survive a surprising amount of cold weather, among them pindo palm, dwarf palmetto, sabal palm, needle palm and Washington palm. If you are in an area that is not frost-free and want tropical palms in your landscape, place them where they receive protection from sheltering trees, buildings, walls or fences, or keep small palms in containers that can be moved indoors when frost threatens.

Planting and Caring for Palms

Most palms prefer slightly sandy, well-drained soil. It allows their roots to "breathe." If your chosen planting site is low-lying, so that the soil is mucky and water puddles there, you may want to add sandy soil to build it up higher, channel water elsewhere, pick another spot, or pick another type of palm (see above).

It is usually more economical to buy seedlings than full-grown palms. However, if the species you desire is a slow grower, you may have to wait a very long time to get the look you're after. There are a few palms that are extremely difficult to transplant full-grown, and therefore must be raised from nursery-grown seedlings. Among these are dwarf palmetto, saw palmetto, and king palm. The best time to plant seedlings is late spring or early summer, because then there is no chance of frost and summer rains will water your plants, so you won't have to.

Most species of palms can be purchased partly or fully grown, "bagged and burlapped." The portion of the root retained on transplanted palms is usually rather small, extending only a foot or two from the trunk. This makes mature palms much easier to transplant than, say, mature oak trees. However, these small rootballs don't do much to anchor palms and they are by nature top heavy. For this reason, newly-transplanted palm trees should be braced by three or more sturdy supports placed around the trunk. The trunk should be padded to protect it and the supports attached to the trunk and staked into the ground. The supports must be sturdy enough to keep the palm upright in a strong wind. When transplanting mature palms, most nurserymen recommend pruning away some or all of the leaves; this temporarily slows the palm's transpiration until its roots regenerate.

Whether you are planting seedlings or full-grown plants, make the planting hole about $1^1/_2$ times the diameter of the rootball. Plant the palm at the same depth it was growing before it was transplanted. You may elect to amend the soil with organic material and a commercial fertilizer, if it seems very sandy. Most palms will grow fine in sandy soil, but the addition of organic material will make the pH of the soil more neutral and improve its ability to hold moisture. Bank soil into a doughnut-shaped dam around the edge of the planting hole, to form a reservoir for water.

Water palms thoroughly when you first plant them, and again every few days for the first couple of months. Then gradually cut back on the frequency of watering. Except in times of extreme drought most palms, once established, do not require supplemental irrigation in addition to rainfall. Water indoor, container-grown palms only when the soil has dried out.

Although most palms will survive without fertilization, it is advised for best appearance and fastest growth. Underfed palms may develop unattractive "bottlenecks," have yellow, spotted or brown-edged leaves, and they will be weaker and therefore more susceptible to insect, disease, and cold-weather damage. With the exception of a few Florida natives adapted to poor, sandy soil—Florida thatch palm, Florida silver palm, sabal palm, saw and scrub palmettos—palms are moderate to heavy feeders. Fertilize them three times a year: in early spring, summer, and fall. The latest research shows that a 8-4-12 fertilizer is the best for palms. Ideally, it also should have about 4% manganese and magnesium (two elements in which palms are often deficient) as well as other necessary micronutrients.

As is true of most plants, established palms will better withstand frost than seedlings or new transplants. Palms can be protected during a cold snap by covering them with fabric or icing them with a fine spray of water. If frost damage does occur, only the affected leaves or portions of the leaves should be pruned away, and this should be done only after all danger of frost has passed. Severely damaged palms may be helped by the application of a copper-based fungicide. Consult your nurseryman about the proper timing and method of application.

Generally, palms are fairly free of insect and disease problems. Brown, red, or black spots on leaves or fruit are the most common signs of trouble. The best way to identify the source of a problem is to take an affected leaf or fruit to your nurseryman or Cooperative Extension Service office for diagnosis and recommended action. When treating any horticultural problem, be conscious of your effect on the environment. It is always a good policy to start with the most benign method of treatment, proceeding to more drastic, ecologically-hostile measures only when absolutely necessary. If, for example, you observe insects attacking your favorite plant, you might first try picking them off by hand and squashing them. If that doesn't work, try blasting them off with a water hose, spraying with cayenne pepper spray, rotenone, insecticidal soap (or even dish soap), or using a biological control like predatory wasps or ladybugs. If

Don't do this! Palms need their green fronds to make food. This sabal palm has been "harsh pruned" and may suffer nutrient deficiencies and wind damage as a result.

all these tactics fail, then you might resort to using chemical controls. But even then, ask questions, read pesticide labels, follow directions carefully, and pick a treatment that seems least damaging. Some palms are susceptible to an incurable disease called "lethal yellowing" carried by leaf hopper bugs. Affected palms drop their fruit and develop yellow, wilting leaves. They may languish sickly for awhile or quickly go into decline and die. The only solution is to replace them with a more resistant palm species. Palms that are very susceptible include triangle, fishtail, Chinese fan, areca, Christmas, Fiji fan and *Phoenix* palms.

Dead fronds may be removed to improve a palm's appearance. Some species tend to look messy and unsightly without regular trimmings. But it does not hurt a palm to let fronds remain until they fall off by themselves. In fact, too little trimming is much healthier for a palm than too much. "Harsh pruning" is performed—unwisely—by many landscape maintenance contractors and uninformed homeowners. Canary Island date palms and sabal palms seem to be the most frequent targets of this destructive practice. Harsh pruning removes not only dead fronds but lower, healthy green fronds. Because the green fronds produce food for the palm via photosynthesis, removing them steals the palm's source of nutrients and may stunt the palm's growth. Undernourished palms are prone to develop weakened and unattractive bottleneck trunks, making them more prone to wind damage. Overpruning also increases vulnerability to frost damage.

Tall palms may be very difficult for the homeowner to trim, and although special long-handled pruning saws are available for the purpose, it often makes excellent sense to engage a professional tree service to trim very large palms.

Palm Gallery

As often happens when suckers are not continually removed from around the base, this cluster of palms has formed upper and lower canopies of leaves.

Both birds and people find the reddish-orange fruit of the Everglades palm attractive, but only birds eat it.

Everglades Palm

In recent years this palm has become very popular in landscaping because it is attractive, native to Florida, as well as being flood, drought, and salt resistant. Although a relatively slow grower, it will eventually reach about 25 feet in height.

Also known as: Saw cabbage, paurotis palm.

Scientific name: *Acoelorraphe wrightii*, named after American botanist Charles Wright.

Native to: Central and south Florida to Central America.

Look for: Very round, fan-shaped leaves, green on top and silvery underneath, up to 3 feet in diameter; leaflets split at the tips; slender, clustered, fiber-covered trunks, reddish-brown or gray, with old leaf bases attached.

Blossom: Panicles of greenish-white flowers grow on flower-stalks which protrude from among the leaves in spring, with both male and female flowers on the same tree.

Fruit: Round, pea-sized fruit is orange when immature, ripens to black or bluish-black; inedible.

Cultivation: Will survive short periods of drought, but requires moist soil for best growth and appearance. Fairly cold hardy and very salt tolerant, it is frequently planted in medians or in a row to act as a screen. Plant in partial or full sun and fertilize at least annually. Some people prefer to remove the suckers that appear around the base. Give it lots of room, as this clustering palm tends to spread outward.

Though Christmas palm is a single-trunked palm, it is often planted in clusters of two or three, as shown here. Its red fruit is produced during the winter months in the northern hemisphere, giving it one of its common names.

Christmas Palm

This small palm has a neat, compact appearance and showy red fruit. It is very popular as a specimen palm, planted around the foundations of buildings, in flowerbeds, or even in large containers on patios or indoors, as it will tolerate some shade.

Also known as: Adonidia palm, Manila palm

Scientific name: *Adonidia merrillii*, after Elmer D. Merrill, director of the New York Botanical Garden from 1929–1935.

Native to: Philippine Islands

Look for: Single, gray, ringed trunk topped by a short green crownshaft; bright green, arching, feather-shaped leaves; small height, up to 25 feet, but usually about 15 feet.

Blossom: White, male and female flowers are borne on the same branched flowerstalk in late summer and fall.

Fruit: Bright red, glossy fruit is inedible.

Cultivation: Though it is easily damaged by frost and very susceptible to lethal yellowing, this palm has few other problems. It is moderately tolerant of drought and salt and not fussy as to soil type. It requires very little grooming to keep it looking neat, and it can be propagated by seed, which germinates in a month or two.

Its polished green crownshaft, neat appearance, and bright red fruit make the king palm a very nice landscape subject.

King Palm

This tall, graceful palm grows to 80 feet in height. The lower trunk is gray-brown, slender, tapered, and ringed by scars left by the bases of fallen leaves. The upper trunk, or crownshaft, is formed by outer leaf bases and is glossy in appearance. Leaves are feather-shaped, up to 15 feet long, with leaflets that are green above, silver underneath.

Also known as: Alexandra palm.

Scientific name: *Archontophoenix alexandrae,* "majestic palm," named for Princess Alexandra of Denmark, later the Queen Dowager of Great Britain.

Native to: Australia—Queensland and New South Wales.

Look for: Single, ringed trunk topped by a light green crownshaft; feather-shaped leaves with silver undersides.

Blossom: Tiny flowers, white or creamy white, are produced in masses at the base of the crownshaft in late spring or summer. Male and female flowers appear on the same tree.

Fruit: Bright red fruit, 1/2 inch in diameter, appears following the blossoms; it is decorative but inedible.

Cultivation: Prefers rich, well-drained soil in a sunny, frost-free location. Not salt tolerant, but drought-resistant and a fairly fast grower. Leaves may sunburn in very hot weather. May be propagated from seed.

The bismarck palm is a handsome addition to the landscape, but it "needs its space," so plant it at least ten feet from buildings or other trees.

Bismarck Palm

This palm is remarkably similar in appearance to the red and blue latan palms, though it grows much larger (eventually). The bluish-green foliage and stiff, fan-shaped leaves of all of these palms make them interesting additions to a subtropical landscape.

Scientific name: *Bismarckia nobilis,* after Prince Bismarck; the species name means "noble."

Native to: Madagascar.

Look for: Single trunk; large, stiff, fan-shaped, bluish-green, waxy leaves with red edges.

Blossom: Creamy white, borne in spring.

Fruit: Brown fruit is not particularly appealing, is inedible.

Cultivation: This rather slow-growing palm needs a site where it receives partial or full sun and where there is plenty of room for its spreading crown of large leaves. It is very drought tolerant and will withstand light frost, but should not be planted in seaside locations as it is not tolerant of salt. Though relatively undemanding regarding care and soil type, regular fertilization produces fastest growth and best appearance.

Blue-green foliage and bright orange fruit make pindo palm a colorful landscape accent.

Pindo Palm

The pindo palm is easily identified by its arching, bluish- to grayish-green leaves. They grow to lengths of 6 feet or more and have a decidedly arched midrib—in small trees the tips may brush the ground. The trunk is often covered with old leaf bases. The pindo palm grows slowly, eventually reaching a height of 20 feet. It is usually used as an ornamental accent plant.

Also known as: Jelly palm.

Scientific name: *Butia capitata*, the latter meaning "headed."

Native to: South America.

Look for: Gray-green, feather-shaped leaves which start out pointing straight up but then curve back toward the ground; single trunk studded with old leaf-bases.

Blossom: Flowers are small, yellowish or reddish white, appear in spring or early summer. Male and female flowers grow on the same tree.

Fruit: The sweet, edible fruit can be used to make delicious jelly. It ripens in summer, is about an inch long, egg-shaped, orange or yellow.

Cultivation: Plant in full sun, away from buildings or other plantings—it requires a lot of room for its spreading leaves. Very drought resistant and somewhat tolerant of salt spray, it has been called the most cold hardy of the pinnate palms, growing as far north as the Carolinas. Though it can be propagated from seeds, they may require six months or more to germinate.

A bright green leaf of the fishtail palm, showing the unusual arrangement of its leaflets.

The clustering fishtail palm can become quite large and shrubby.

Fishtail Palm

The fishtail palm has a trait unusual in palms: it has compound leaves. Each shiny, green leaflet has a characteristic fishtail shape. This palm grows in a clump, with new suckers constantly coming up from around the base. It is relatively small, reaching 20 to 25 feet in height in subtropical regions of the U.S. A single-trunked relative, C. urens, *is equally nice looking but less desirable for cultivation because it dies a natural death after it has reached the ripe old age of about ten years.*

Scientific name: *Caryota mitis*, meaning "nut," and "mild" or "soft," respectively.

Native to: India and Malaysia.

Look for: Compound leaves with bright green, fishtail-shaped leaflets; dense cluster of slim trunks.

Blossom: Small, white flowers appear in spring in dense clusters among the branches. Male and female flowers are borne on the same tree.

Fruit: Small, bluish-black fruit is definitely inedible, will sting the mouth if eaten. This palm's sap, however, is used to make "jaggery sugar" in its area of origin.

Cultivation: Fishtail palm is not at all salt or cold tolerant, growing only in frost-free areas. It requires fertile, regularly-watered, well-drained soil in a sunny location. It has a moderate growth rate, can be very successfully grown indoors, and may be propagated by transplanting suckers.

No kitty, this isn't a "cat palm"—that's C. cataractum. *It is hardy bamboo palm,* C. microspadix, *which has at least three points in its favor: pretty green foliage, decorative red fruit, and cold hardiness.*

Bamboo Palm

This genus of tropical palms includes single- and multi-trunked varieties, most extremely sensitive to cold and therefore used primarily as house plants. Chamaedorea elegans *has a single trunk and grows to about three feet.* C. cataractarum *and* C. seifrizii *reach heights of 4–8 feet and have multiple trunks that grow in dense clumps.* C. erumpens *is also multi-trunked; it may grow to 10 feet and more often is found growing outdoors in warm areas. The palm pictured at left is an uncharacteristically cold hardy species that can withstand temperatures in the low 20s.*

Also known as: Parlor palm, cat palm, reed palm, neanthe belle.

Scientific name: *Chamaedorea* spp., derived from the Greek words for "dwarf" and "gift."

Native to: Mexico, Central America.

Look for: Small palms, under 10 feet, with narrow, straight trunk or trunks; soft, feather-shaped leaves with tapered, widely-spaced leaflets.

Blossom: Male and female flowers appear in summertime, grow on separate plants. Flowers are small, yellow or creamy white, and delicate.

Fruit: Small, globular, red, orange, reddish-orange or black; inedible.

Cultivation: Require deep shade for best leaf color. Most are commonly grown as house plants. Prefer fertile, well-drained soil, grow slowly to moderately. Most species will not tolerate frost, they are not salt tolerant, and they require regular watering.

Trim away old, dead fronds to give European fan palm its best appearance—but be careful of its sharp, orange spines!

European Fan Palm

Due to its small size, this palm is best used as a garden or patio specimen, planted in the ground or a large container. It is also eye-pleasing planted in a group as a lawn accent. If placed in a sunny exposure, it also makes a nice foundation planting.

Also known as: Mediterranean fan palm.

Scientific name: *Chamaerops humilis*, meaning "dwarf bush."

Native to: Mediterranean region of Europe.

Look for: Height usually under 15 feet; stiff, fan-shaped, green or gray-green leaves. Leaf tips do not droop as in the Chinese fan palm. Usually single-trunked, but sometimes develops multiple trunks from suckers that come up around the base.

Blossom: Inconspicuous flowers are borne in dense clusters among the foliage during the spring season. Male and female flowers are usually produced on different trees, although they do sometimes occur on the same plant.

Fruit: Red or yellow berries are inconspicuous, globular in shape, inedible.

Cultivation: A very slow grower, this palm needs regular watering to thrive, but it will survive short periods of drought. Cold hardy, it grows as far north as the Carolinas but is only moderately salt tolerant. Plant in sun or partial shade, fertilize lightly in spring and summer, and remove grass and weeds from underneath. May be propagated by transplanting suckers, or by seed.

C. argentata, *the Florida silver palm.*

Hispaniolan silver palm, C. argentea, *also has fan-shaped leaves with silvery backs, but its leaves are stiffer. It is native to the Caribbean Islands. Like its close relative the Florida silver palm, it is drought and salt tolerant, but cannot stand frost.*

Florida Silver Palm

This native palm is ideally suited for south Florida and coastal central Florida. It is very drought and salt tolerant and will withstand some frost, but only when placed in a protected location. It grows very slowly but requires no care, thriving without fertilizer and with very little water.

Scientific name: *Coccothrinax argentata*, meaning "three-pronged seed" and "silver," respectively.

Native to: South Florida and the Bahamas.

Look for: Single-trunked palm, growing to 15 feet in height; pretty, fan-shaped leaves, deeply divided between leaflets, dull green above, silvery white and scaly underneath; layers of fiber surround the uppermost part of the slender, gray trunk.

Blossom: Small white flowers have both male and female components, are borne in the summer on flowerstalks which emerge from among the leaves.

Fruit: Dark brown, inedible fruit.

Cultivation: Requires very little care, but needs sandy, well-drained soil. Plant in a sunny location and forget. May be propagated by seeds.

Because it is so often used in advertising as a symbol of tropical splendor and relaxation, the coconut palm is easily recognizable to most people. Its fruit (below) has a green fibrous hull that hides a round, brown nut containing delicious coconut meat and milk.

Coconut Palm

Strictly a tropical tree, the coconut is best suited to the southernmost parts of Florida, from Fort Myers southward. The variety known as the dwarf Malayan coconut has a shorter, straighter trunk and bears golden-yellow fruit.

Scientific name: *Cocos nucifera. Cocos* is Portuguese for monkey, referring to the "face" on the nut. *Nucifera* means "nut-bearing."

Native to: Origin uncertain, because it has become naturalized throughout the tropics.

Look for: Curving, ringed, gray trunk, to 80 feet in height, usually inclined; sweeping, feathery, yellowish-green leaves; large green or golden-yellow fruits.

Blossom: Waxy yellowish-white flowers are borne year round, on flowerstalks which emerge from within two- to three-foot long spathes. One tree produces both male and female flowers. The flowerstalks contain a sweet substance called toddy which is used for sugar or distilled to make alcohol.

Fruit: The well-known coconut, source of sweet, white meat and milk. Nuts require 9 to 10 months to mature, and are not produced until a tree is 5 to 10 years old.

Cultivation: Because its floating nuts naturally propagate along shorelines, the coconut palm has developed complete salt tolerance. It is also drought tolerant, but will not withstand cold weather; a hard freeze killed virtually all of the coconut trees in south Florida in 1958. Propagated by seed.

Hurricane palm adds a feeling of the islands to its surroundings. It is admired for its pretty green foliage and crownshaft.

Hurricane Palm

This tropical palm makes a lovely specimen plant in the garden. Its common name comes from its superb resistance to wind.

Also known as: Princess palm.

Scientific name: *Dictyosperma album*, meaning "netted-seed" and white, respectively.

Native to: Mascarene Islands, located in the Indian Ocean off the western coast of Madagascar.

Look for: Single, straight, gray trunk with rings left by old leaves; light green crownshaft; height to 30 feet; bright green, feather-shaped leaves, 8–12 feet in length.

Blossom: Yellowish-white flowers are borne in spring.

Fruit: Round fruit is half an inch in length, deep purplish-black when ripe, inedible.

Cultivation: This palm cannot survive cold weather, but it is moderately tolerant of both salt spray and drought. It needs full sun and regular fertilization for best appearance, and it grows rather slowly.

Above, a triangle palm provides the focal point for a fountain at the palm garden in the Florida Botanical Gardens in Largo, a stunning example of its use as a specimen planting. At right, you can see from the triangular configuration of the leaf bases why this palm has its common name; also notice the flowerstalk just beginning to emerge from among the leaves.

Triangle Palm

Though the triangle palm is endangered in its home of Madagascar, it is a prized landscape subject elsewhere. Its most characteristic trait is the arrangement of its leaves, the leaf bases giving the trunk a roughly triangular shape.

Scientific name: *Dypsis decaryi*, named in honor of the botanist/ethnologist Raymond Decary, who studied the flora of the island of Madagascar and its people.

Native to: Madagascar.

Look for: Stocky, triangular, solitary trunk with no true crownshaft. Upright, stiff, pinnate leaves up to 10 feet long. Leaflets are bluish to gray-green, with the lowest ones dangling almost to the ground. Underside of leaves and leaf bases have reddish scales or hairs. Mature palms may reach 25 feet.

Blossom: Male and female flowers are borne on the same inflorescence. Yellow flowers are borne in spring on a branched flowerstalk that emerges from among the lower leaves.

Fruit: Yellowish-green fruit is about an inch long, is harvested for food in Madagascar.

Cultivation: Suitable for frost-free areas only. Adaptable to any well-drained soil. Drought tolerant once established. Prefers full sun. Slight susceptibility to lethal yellowing. May be propagated by seed.

Improve the appearance of areca palm by removing the suckers around the base every so often, to show off its green, bamboo-like stems.

Areca Palm

This is a beautiful cluster palm, often used as a patio specimen, house plant, or foundation accent. If planted in central Florida, it must be located in a protected, frost-free location. Related species are D. cabadae *(red fruit) and* D. madagascarensis *(single trunk).*

Also known as: Butterfly palm, cane palm.

Scientific name: *Dypsis lutescens*, referring to its yellowish fruit.

Native to: Madagascar.

Look for: Multiple, slender trunks with light-colored rings resembling those on bamboo; yellowish-green crownshaft; yellowish-green, erect, feather-like leaves; height to about 15 feet.

Blossom: Small white flowers are borne in spring on branched flowerstalks which grow out from the base of the crownshaft. Male and female flowers are produced on different trees.

Fruit: Inch-long, dark purple or black, oblong fruit is relished by birds and other wildlife.

Cultivation: Prefers a rich, acidic, well-drained soil. Fertilize regularly to prevent overly yellow foliage. A sunny location is needed for steady growth, though it will tolerate shade, as evidenced by its frequent use as a house plant. Must be protected from frost and salt air. Somewhat tolerant of drought. Usually cultivated by division.

Spindle palm (flowerstalk at right) and bottle palm (below) draw curious looks; they are used by most people as specimen plants, collected for their interesting trunk shapes.

©1995 Mark Issenberg

Bottle Palm

Two species of this palm genus, desired for their unusual trunks, are grown in Florida. Hyophorbe lagenicaulis, *bottle palm, has a bulge at the bottom of the trunk and a very short leaf stem with a yellow stripe on the underside; its leaves have a distinctive lateral twist.* H. verschaffeltii, *spindle palm, has a bulge in the center of the trunk and a longer, reddish-colored leaf stem with no yellow stripe; Spindle palm leaves are not twisted.*

Scientific name: *Hyophorbe lagenicaulis*, the latter meaning "bottle-stemmed."

Native to: Mascarene Islands.

Look for: Gray trunk that bulges out at the bottom; feather-shaped, downcurved leaves, 18–30 inches long and twisted looking; relatively few leaves in crown; height to 25 feet.

Blossom: Small white flowers are borne in summer on stalks which emerge from the base of the green crownshaft. Male and female flowers appear on the same tree.

Fruit: Small (less than an inch in length), black, oblong, rough-surfaced, inedible.

Cultivation: Requires full sun and well-drained, fertile soil. Not tolerant of cold, but very salt tolerant and somewhat drought tolerant. Feed this slow-growing tree several times a year with a palm fertilizer.

Although its fruit (right) isn't particularly attractive, the red latan palm's silvery-blue foliage adds a nice touch to the garden.

Red Latan Palm

This unusual-looking palm makes a nice specimen plant, either in the yard or along a street or driveway. Though slow-growing, its canopy of leaves spreads 12 feet or more when it is still fairly young, so put it in a location where it has plenty of room. L. loddigesii, *the blue latan palm, is very similar; its leaves have a more bluish cast.*

Scientific name: *Latania lontaroides.*

Native to: Mascarene Islands.

Look for: Rigid, grayish-green, fan-shaped leaves, 6–8 feet across; red veins along the edges of leaves and leaf stems; a waxy coating on leaves; single trunk, slightly enlarged at the base; height to 30 feet.

Blossom: Yellowish-white, male and female flowers grow on different plants. They are borne in summer, on stalks emerging from among the leaves.

Fruit: Dark brown, 1–2 inches long, round, inedible.

Cultivation: Slow-growing, will survive light frost. Very drought resistant, but not salt tolerant. Requires full sun in a well-drained area.

Droopy, fan-shaped leaves are the most obvious identifying feature of the Chinese fan palm. Fruit (right) is inedible.

Chinese Fan Palm

The Chinese fan palm is a lovely tree for many landscape uses. The most widely planted of the Livistona *genus, it may be seen in many places around the state of Florida. Other species are Australian fan palm,* L. australis *(very cold hardy) and footstool palm,* L. rotundifolia *(a good indoor palm, also known as round-leaf fan palm).*

Scientific name: *Livistona chinensis*, the former to honor the founder of Edinburgh Botanic Garden (born in Livistone, Scotland) and the latter for its country of origin.

Native to: China.

Look for: Drooping leaf tips, especially on older trees; ringed, single trunk, sometimes having old leaf bases attached; glossy, dark green, fan-shaped leaves, deeply divided between leaflets; each leaflet has a prominent yellow nerve along the center; leaf stems have saw-toothed edges; height to 30 feet.

Blossom: Borne on long flowerstalks which emerge from among the leaves, with male and female flowers appearing on the same tree; flowers are yellowish-white and appear in summer.

Fruit: Bluish-black when ripe, up to an inch long, oblong, resembling an olive; inedible.

Cultivation: This slow-growing palm may be cultivated indoors as a container plant in well-lighted areas, or outside in partial to full sun. It is not particular as to soil type, is very drought resistant, cold hardy throughout Florida and in southern California, but is not tolerant of salt. May be grown from seed.

Colorful flowerstalks, flowers and fruit (left) are among the desirable qualities of this popular palm.

Its location a few feet from the waters of Tampa Bay attests to the salt tolerance of this Canary Island date palm (below).

Canary Island Date Palm

The Canary Island date palm is truly regal looking. The beauty of some specimens is enhanced by the growth of ferns on the trunk, in the crevices formed by old leaf bases. Some people also place flowers, epiphytes, or orchids on the trunks of large trees. All palms in the Phoenix *genus have a tendency to hybridize with each other, producing trees with a mixture of characteristics.*

Also known as: Pineapple palm, because of its rotund appearance and resemblance to a pineapple when young.

Scientific name: *Phoenix canariensis*, the former being the Greek word for palm, the latter indicating its place of origin.

Native to: Canary Islands, off the northwest coast of Africa.

Look for: Stout, barrel-shaped trunk covered with old leaf bases or scars; long, recurving, tapered, feather-shaped leaves with stiff, spiny leaflets; leaflets folded into their stems with edges turned upward; portion of petiole without leaflets is short; sharp spikes at the base of each leaf stem; height to 40 feet.

Blossom: Male and female flowers are borne on different plants. Yellow flowers are borne in spring on branched flowerstalks emerging from among leaves.

Fruit: Bright orange, egg-shaped fruits are produced in large clusters on female trees. Each is about one inch in diameter. They are edible, but unpalatable.

Cultivation: Its spreading, spiny branches dictate that this palm be planted away from buildings and footpaths. Needs full sun; fertilize regularly to prevent yellow foliage. This palm is drought resistant, moderately salt tolerant and cold hardy, but it grows rather slowly when young.

Edible Date Palm

Even if they never bear fruit, date palms are a lovely addition to the landscape, with their interesting, textured trunks and feathery fronds. They're excellent for a park or large yard, and a row of them along a street looks very elegant. The cultivar 'Medjool' has been bred to produce better quality, larger fruit.

Scientific name: *Phoenix dactylifera*, "finger-bearing palm."

Native to: Middle East.

Look for: Sparse crown of straight, grayish-green, feather-shaped leaves, up to 20 feet in length; slender, single trunk with geometric pattern formed by old leaf bases; suckers around the base of the trunk, dissipating somewhat with age; portion of petiole without leaflets may be as much as one-third of the length of the leaf; height to 70 feet.

Blossom: Fragrant white flowers grow on long, branched flowerstalks which emerge from among the leaves. Male and female flowers are produced in spring, on separate trees. Consequently, both a male and a female tree are needed to produce fruit.

Fruit: The well-known commercial date. It is oblong, up to 3 inches in length, deep orange when ripe and very sweet, containing as much as 60 per cent sugar.

Cultivation: As you would expect of a tree native to arid places like Egypt and North Africa, this palm is exceptionally tolerant of dry weather. It is cold hardy, resistant to salt, grows moderately fast, and prefers full sun. Grown commercially for its fruit in California, it may also bear fruit elsewhere if well cared for and adequately fertilized.

The origin of the species name "reclinata" is obvious when you compare the gracefully curving trunk of this Senegal date palm with the straight trunks of the other palms growing nearby.

Senegal Date Palm

This appealing cluster palm is frequently used in landscaping. It is often seen planted in medians, as a central focal point for a large flowerbed, or as a free-standing specimen. Although it grows slowly, it can become quite large. Plant it away from buildings, since its cluster of trunks require considerable room. It has a greater tendency to escape from cultivation than other Phoenix *species.*

Scientific name: *Phoenix reclinata*, "reclining palm."

Native to: Central Africa.

Look for: Multiple trunks growing from a central point; individual trunks leaning at an angle, usually free from old leaf bases but bearing their scars and covered with reddish-brown fiber; bright, glossy green, recurving, feather-shaped leaves, with stiff, spiny leaflets; height to 35 feet.

Blossom: Small white flowers appear in spring, growing on short, branched flowerstalks. Each emerges from among the leaves, covered by a boat-shaped spathe. Male and female flowers grow on separate trees.

Fruit: Small, egg-shaped dates are reddish-brown or orange, attractive, produced on female trees only; inedible.

Cultivation: Requires full sun but is otherwise undemanding as to care. Although slow growing, this palm is cold hardy, somewhat salt tolerant, and very resistant to drought. Periodically remove the suckers which come up from around the base—if they are allowed to grow, the tree will eventually become an impenetrable clump of sharp, spiny leaves. Plant well away from sidewalks and footpaths.

Pygmy date palm can be grown either in partial shade or full sun. Often, several are planted toether to form a cluster. Its petite size makes it desirable for use in small suburban yards. Its flowers (left) are a pretty yellow color, but are not fragrant or particularly showy.

Pygmy Date Palm

This palm is widely cultivated for its fine, feathery foliage and small size. Its rough trunk resembles that of its larger relative, the edible date palm. In addition to being an excellent container plant, it is frequently planted in medians, looks especially nice when planted in groups or used to frame an entryway; it makes a good focal point for a flowerbed, and it's an excellent foundation planting.

Scientific name: *Phoenix roebelenii*, named for Carl Roebelen, a plant collector who first discovered the palm in Laos.

Native to: Southeast Asia.

Look for: Single-trunked, dwarf palm, to 15 feet; slender trunk, usually rough and spiny looking; finely cut, feather-shaped, dark green, arching leaves; weak spines on leaf bases.

Blossom: Short, branched flowerstalk has small, yellowish-white flowers. Male and female flowers are produced in spring, on different trees.

Fruit: Very small, oblong, dark-colored fruit is inedible.

Cultivation: Grows well in partial to full sun. Mature specimens will withstand some frost. Slow growing, it is excellent as an indoor or outdoor potted plant. It will survive short periods of drought, but is not salt tolerant.

The big leaves of Fiji fan palm (right) are its most noticeable feature. They make it stand out from other nearby foliage in the garden (below).

Fiji Fan Palm

This tropical palm is tender and will grow only in subtropical and tropical areas free from very cold weather. Its huge, deeply folded leaves make it an interesting accent plant. Choose a site protected from strong winds, as they may damage the leaves. Fiji fan palm's close relative P. thurstonii, though also a tropical tree, is slightly more tolerant of cold temperatures and has six-foot long flowerstalks that hang down below the crown of leaves.

Also known as: Pritchardia palm.

Scientific name: *Pritchardia pacifica,* named for W. T. Pritchard, the British Consul to Fiji in 1860.

Native to: Pacific Islands.

Look for: Height to 30 feet; very stiff, fan-shaped, green leaves with undivided leaflets; single, smooth, grey trunk.

Blossom: Pendulous flowerstalks emerge from among the leaves in summer; at the end of each is a cluster of tiny, brownish-yellow flowers.

Fruit: Tiny, round, black fruit is inedible.

Cultivation: This slow-growing palm is moderately salt tolerant and drought resistant, but it will not survive cold weather. It may be propagated from seed, and should be placed in well-drained, fertile soil in a sunny or partly sunny spot.

Above left, the flowerstalk of the buccaneer palm. Above right, closeup of flowers and immature fruits. At left, a mature palm at Gizella Kopsick Palm Arboretum in St. Petersburg. It is about 8 feet tall.

Buccaneer Palm

This petite palm is an ideal specimen for a small garden. It is native to the Caribbean and the Florida Keys. Its bluish-green, feathery foliage, pale green crownshaft, yellow flowers and beautiful red fruit make it a colorful landscape subject in all seasons.

Also known as: Sargent's cherry palm.

Scientific Name: *Pseudophoenix sargentii*, after its discoverer, Charles Sprague Sargent, and for its presumed resemblance to *Phoenix* palms.

Native to: Florida Keys and Caribbean Islands.

Look for: Small height, to 10 feet; arching, feather-shaped, bluish- or gray-green leaves; gray, ringed single trunk topped by light bluish-green crownshaft.

Blossom: Yellow flowers are borne on a flowerstalk that emerges from among the leaves.

Fruit: Red, inedible fruit is about ¾" in diameter.

Cultivation: This palm is very slow-growing and not at all tolerant of frost, but these are its only shortcomings. It is extremely tolerant of drought, salt and pests, is adaptable to different soil types, needs little or no fertilizer, and will grow in full sun to partial shade. It may be propagated by seed.

This little solitaire palm has sustained a bit of freeze damage, but with the return of warm weather and a little tender loving care it will recover. The large palms in the background are Sabals.

Solitaire Palm

Solitaire palms look very nice when planted alone or in groups of two or three on a lawn. Their shiny green crownshafts, arched leaves and bright, berry-like fruits make them especially sought-after as ornamental landscape subjects.

Scientific name: *Ptychosperma elegans*, meaning "folded seed" and "elegant," respectively.

Native to: Queensland, Australia.

Look for: Arched, erect, feather-shaped leaves; wide, bright green leaflets; single, slender, straight, prominently ringed trunk surmounted by a slender, bright green crownshaft; a small tree, with a maximum height of 15-20 feet; usually has fairly few leaves at one time, somewhere between 6 and 20, depending on tree size.

Blossom: Large clusters of small, white flowers are produced in summer, on branched flowerstalks which emerge from the base of the crownshaft. Male and female flowers grow on the same tree.

Fruit: Very showy, bright red fruits are slightly oblong and very small, less than an inch in diameter. They are inedible.

Cultivation: Slow-growing, not salt tolerant, and tender, this palm is best suited to subtropical regions. It is moderately resistant to drought but prefers regular irrigation. Plant in a sunny location, fertilize three times a year.

©James Phillips/Silverlake Photography

Majesty Palm

The majesty palm has come into widespread favor as a landscape subject only very recently. It is a decorative specimen palm that will likely increase in popularity as more people become familiar with it.

Scientific name: *Ravenea rivularis*, the latter meaning "brook-loving."

Native to: Madagascar.

Look for: Single trunk, very light in color, slightly enlarged near the center and tapering upward; dark green, feather-shaped leaves covered with a white, cottony down, about 5 feet long; somewhat resembles the royal palm, but is taller and has no green crownshaft.

Blossom: Male and female flowers are produced on separate trees, within downy-covered spathes.

Fruit: Small, red, globular fruits are inedible.

Cultivation: Though it grows in swampy places near freshwater rivers in its native habitat, the majesty palm is moderately drought and salt resistant. It will tolerate some cold weather, growing as far north as Orlando, Florida. Although frost may cause cosmetic damage to foliage, the tree will survive and generate new leaves. It's a rather heavy feeder, especially when placed in full sun, so fertilize it faithfully.

An understory plant, needle palm prefers moist, shady areas. It gets its name from the sharp needle-like spines that protrude from its fiber-covered trunk. The specimen pictured here was photographed in Torreya State Park in the Florida Panhandle.

Needle Palm

This endangered, very slow-growing palm has dark green, deeply divided leaves. Although it is very drought tolerant, its natural habitats are wet: shady hammocks near swamps or mesic forests.

Scientific name: *Rhapidophyllum hystrix*, from the Greek words for "needle," "leaf" and "porcupine," respectively.

Native to: Southeastern United States.

Look for: Single, short trunk, loosely covered with a tangled mass of dark brownish to blackish fiber; palmate leaves with deeply divided leaflets, dark green above, silvery below; smooth petiole; sharp, black, needle-like spines up to 8 inches long protruding from the trunk, from among the leaf bases.

Blossom: Yellow, insignificant flowers are borne on stems up to a foot in length; male and female flowers usually are produced on different plants.

Fruit: Inch-long, purplish-brown, woolly, egg-shaped. Black bears have been known to eat it.

Cultivation: Needle palm is an excellent low-maintenance landscape choice for partial sun to deep shade. It is so slow-growing that it rarely needs trimming and it's not particular as to soil type. Though it benefits from occasional fertilization and regular irrigation, it's very drought resistant once established and also somewhat salt tolerant. It never gets very large, topping out at about 5 feet in height, with a diameter of perhaps 10 feet. Frost tolerant, it grows as far north as Zone 8 but occurs naturally as far south as Highlands County, Florida and has been cultivated on down into the Florida Keys. It may be propagated by seed or by division of clumps.

Wide leaves with blunt tips are characteristic of broadleaf lady palm. For best leaf color, plant it in a partly sunny location.

Broadleaf Lady Palm

This low-growing cluster palm makes a nice informal hedge. It also can be used in planters, as a foundation plant, or indoors as a house plant. It forms dense, rounded clumps of leaves. Yellow-leaved and variegated cultivars have been developed for the nursery trade.

Scientific name: *Rhapis excelsa*, the former from the Greek word for needle, the latter meaning "tall."

Native to: China.

Look for: Palm-shaped leaves, each with 5 to 10 leaflets about an inch wide, widely spaced, and separated all the way to the stem; finely serrated leaf edge and blunt, almost square, leaf tips; multiple, slender trunks that grow upright in a tight cluster; smooth, green, cane-like trunk, the top portion covered with brown fiber; height to 8 feet.

Blossom: Small, branched flowerstalks are borne at the tip ends of the trunks in summer, and have insignificant white or yellowish-white flowers. Male and female flowers are borne on different plants.

Fruit: Very tiny, dark colored, oblong fruit is inedible.

Cultivation: The lady palm resembles a shrub more than a tree, considering its low profile and clustering habit. It grows slowly, is somewhat salt and drought resistant, and is surprisingly cold hardy. A light frost may burn the leaves, but the plant usually survives. Lady palm prefers a partially shady location and is a very popular container plant, either indoors or on the patio. It has moderate nutritional needs, but in poor or alkaline soils supplemental iron and manganese may be required for best color and fastest growth.

These two royal palms at Sarasota Jungle Gardens dwarf all the other palms around them. Note their immense, gray, solid-looking trunks.

Royal Palm

A row of these beautiful palms in a park or along a boulevard is simply stunning, and on windy days the sound of their rustling fronds is delightful. For a tropical look, they're hard to beat. Florida and Cuban royal palms were once considered to be distinct, but botanists are now grouping them together in a single species.

Scientific name: *Roystonea regia*, for American engineer Roy Stone; "regia" is Latin for royal.

Native to: Florida Everglades, Cuba.

Look for: Tall, straight, cement-gray trunk, slightly bulged in the center; bright, glossy-green crownshaft; sweeping, feather-shaped, shiny green leaves, to 10 feet long and 6 feet wide; height may reach 50–125 feet.

Blossom: Male and female flowers grow on the same tree; yellow flowers are produced in spring on yard-long, branched flowerstalks which are covered by spathes and emerge from the base of the crownshaft.

Fruit: Purplish, oblong fruit is ¼ inch in diameter; inedible to humans but eaten by birds.

Cultivation: A native of swampy places, royal palm likes moist, fertile soil. Because even established trees will tolerate only light frost, this palm should be planted only in south Florida. Though not salt tolerant, it will withstand short periods of drought. In full sun and with regular watering it will grow moderately fast.

Scrub palmetto is almost always trunkless. In springtime, its clusters of white flowers attract pollinating insects and in fall birds feast on its berries. It is very resistant to the lightning-sparked fires that are regular occurrences during the summer in central Florida scrub, resprouting within just a few days.

Scrub Palmetto

This shrubby palm is endemic to Florida scrub, which occurs on sandy, well-drained ridges along the central spine of the state and on the coasts in a number of places. It is a low- to no-care choice for full sun in mixed borders and foundation plantings. Scrub palmetto's extreme drought tolerance makes it an ideal choice for the natural zone of Xeriscape gardens.

Scientific name: *Sabal etonia.*

Native to: Florida's Lake Wales Ridge and coastal scrubs.

Look for: Shrubby habit, usually trunkless, rarely developing a very short, thick trunk; deeply divided, fan-shaped leaves; costapalmate leaves like those of the sabal palm; stiff, green leaves; height to about 6 feet.

Blossom: Male and female flowers grow on the same plant; flowers are white, appear in spring, growing from a short flowerstalk that does not extend beyond the leaves.

Fruit: Small, dark brown, oblong and fleshy; inedible to people but eaten by birds and other wildlife.

Cultivation: Very slow-growing, but virtually carefree. Will grow in almost any well-drained soil, is cold hardy, extremely drought resistant, and fairly salt tolerant. Prefers full sun but will tolerate partial shade. Extremely difficult to transplant, so start seeds or buy small container-grown seedlings.

The dwarf palmetto is almost always trunkless, and is often mistaken for an immature sabal palm, which it strongly resembles. The leaves of both species are "costapalmate" (fan-shaped, and having a midrib), but the leaflets of dwarf palmetto stand up straighter than those of the sabal palm, whose leaves appear to be folded in half and have a characteristic downward twist.

Dwarf Palmetto

Although the dwarf palmetto and the scrub palmetto are very similar in appearance, they live in habitats that are totally different. While scrub palmetto thrives in dry, sandy soil in full sun, dwarf palmetto's preferred habitat is in partial shade in moist forests and fertile bottomlands. If you're going for a natural look in your yard, dwarf palmettos are a nice choice. Use them to soften entranceways, plant them under and around stands of trees, or fill planters with them.

Also known as: Blue palm, bluestem palmetto

Scientific name: *Sabal minor*, "small sabal palm."

Native to: Southeastern U.S.: coastal North Carolina to Texas.

Look for: Shrubby habit, usually trunkless, rarely developing a very short, thick trunk; deeply divided, fan-shaped leaves; costapalmate leaves have an extremely short midrib; stiff, green or bluish-green leaves; height to about 6 feet.

Blossom: Male and female flowers grow on the same plant; flowers are white, appear in summer, grow from a very long, erect stalk.

Fruit: About ⅓" in diameter, round, black and shiny, inedible to people but eaten by birds and mammals.

Cultivation: Very easy to care for. Will grow in almost any soil, is very cold hardy, moderately salt tolerant and surprisingly drought resistant. It is evergreen, prefers partial sun or light shade. Extremely difficult to transplant, so start seeds or buy small container-grown seedlings.

Sabal palms grow so slowly (about 4 inches per year) that even medium-sized ones like those shown above are very old. Most of those used in commercial, residential and municipal landscaping have been collected from wild populations of trees. Because they seem ubiquitous, most people take them for granted, but they are a valuable natural resource and deserve reasonable protection measures. The flowerstalks that bear their pale yellow, lacy flowers can be quite large and very showy, as on the tree at left.

Sabal Palm

This palm is the one most commonly seen in Florida, and is the state tree of Florida and South Carolina. Its trunk sometimes has old leaf bases, or "boots," surrounding all or part of it, making an interesting criss-cross pattern. If you're looking for an eye-pleasing, carefree palm, this tree is for you.

Also known as: Cabbage palm, because early Florida crackers ate the palm hearts in "swamp cabbage salad," a harvest that was lethal to the palm, unfortunately.

Scientific name: *Sabal palmetto*, the species name meaning "little palm."

Native to: Florida and the coasts of the Carolinas.

Look for: Fan-shaped leaves with a midrib which gives them a characteristic, twisted appearance; pointed, droopy leaf segments with threads hanging between them; green or bluish-green leaflets divided about one-third of the way from tip to base; single, gray, straight trunk; height to 90 feet.

Blossom: Sweetly fragrant, white flowers have both male and female components; they grow on a flowerstalk which emerges from among leaves; may appear from spring through fall. Very attractive to pollinating insects.

Fruit: Shiny, black, round, tiny, and inedible to humans.

Cultivation: In its native range, this palm grows with absolutely no care. It thrives in the sandiest soil, surviving drought and cold weather and ignoring salt spray. The only requirement is lots of light, but even in full sun this palm is very slow growing. Too many people overtrim these palms; they need a full crown of leaves for healthy growth.

Saw palmetto is endemic
throughout the southeastern
United States. The blue form
(right) is prized as a landscape subject.

Saw Palmetto

This palmetto is common in Florida and coastal Georgia and South Carolina, where it forms huge colonies. It is very resistant to fire, and though it may appear to have been destroyed, soon green shoots will appear from the charred remains of the trunks. The leaves sometimes have a distinct bluish cast to them, especially in those plants growing near the Atlantic coast.

Scientific name: *Serenoa repens*, genus named for American botanist Sereno Watson, the species name meaning "creeping."

Native to: South Carolina to the Florida Keys.

Look for: Reddish-brown, fiber-covered trunk, growing upright or prostrate along the ground for 10 feet or more; deeply cleft, fan-shaped leaves ranging in color from yellow-green to blue-green; saw-toothed edges on leaflets; rarely exceeds 10 feet in height.

Blossom: Fragrant white flowers have both male and female components, are borne on creeping, branched stalks which grow from the base of the plant in summer.

Fruit: Black or bluish-black fruit is small, pear-shaped, inedible to humans, but eaten by birds and animals.

Cultivation: Drought resistant, cold hardy, and salt tolerant. Grows in full sun or partial shade. Mature plants are just about impossible to transplant; buy nursery-grown seedlings.

Queen palm is one of few palms that bloom and bear year round. The palm above has both flowers and unripe fruit. Queen palm is easily propagated and transplanted, and is probably the most common exotic palm in Florida.

Queen Palm

One of the most commonly cultivated palms, this single-trunked species is grown as a street, background or accent tree, either alone or in a group. It looks nice when well cared for, with its long, sweeping, feather-like fronds, which in young trees frequently touch the ground. The trunk is straight, grayish, and ringed. The graceful foliage emerges from a mass of untidy-looking, fibrous leaf-sheaths.

Also known as: Cocos plumosa, feather palm.

Scientific name: *Syagrus romanzoffiana*, the former meaning "wild pig" (name used by the Roman naturalist Pliny for a palm), the latter honoring of Nikolai Romanzoff, a Russian patron of science.

Native to: Central Brazil to Argentina.

Look for: Single, straight, gray, ringed trunk; sweeping, glossy green, feather-shaped leaves; canoe-shaped flower spathes; height to 40 feet.

Blossom: Large clusters of tiny yellow or cream-colored flowers are produced on flowerstalks covered by a heavy, woody spathe which emerges from among the leaves. Both male and female flowers appear on the same tree, are produced year round.

Fruit: Oblong, date-like fruits are orange when ripe, a little over an inch in length; they are edible but not particularly tasty, and can be messy.

Cultivation: A heavy feeder, this palm grows fairly quickly given adequate water and fertilization. Prefers full sun and sandy soil. Not particularly salt tolerant, it will survive light frost but may be killed by a hard freeze. Easily propagated from seed. If not regularly removed, old leaf boots and flower spathes become unsightly.

A Florida thatch palm grows in a shady spot at Marie Selby Botanical Gardens in Sarasota, a bit farther north than its natural range. Its oceanside, protected location has allowed it to survive the cold snaps that hit central Florida every few years.

Thatch Palm

Both Thrinax morrisii *(Key thatch palm) and* Thrinax radiata *(Florida thatch palm) are uncommon, classified as "commercially exploited." A grouping of several of these small palms is lovely as the central focal point of a flowerbed or to soften a stark corner of the garden.*

Also known as: Peaberry palm

Scientific name: *Thrinax* spp., Greek for "fan."

Native to: South Florida, Florida Keys and Caribbean Islands.

Look for: Fan-shaped, nearly circular leaves, about 3 feet across, with green or silver undersides; leaf stems have a reddish-colored base enclosed in wooly fiber and are 2 to 3 feet long; single, straight trunk, to 20 feet in height.

Blossom: Small, yellow flowers have both male and female components, are produced in spring on long flowerstalks which protrude from among the leaves.

Fruit: Shiny, white, pea-sized fruit is relished by wildlife.

Cultivation: Grows very slowly, but needs little care other than an occasional trimming of dead leaves. Though extremely drought resistant and salt tolerant, it is truly a subtropical tree and cannot survive freezing weather. Plant in partial or full sun in well-drained soil.

Montgomery Palm

This lovely palm has beautiful, dark green foliage and inviting red berries in fall. A tropical palm, it may be grown only in frost-free areas.

Also known as: Sunshine palm.

Scientific name: *Veitchia arecina.*

Native to: South Pacific Islands.

Look for: Single, straight, gray, ringed trunk; grayish-green crownshaft; feather-shaped, slightly arched leaves with wide, dark green leaflets, about 10 feet in length; height to 35 feet.

Blossom: White flowers are borne on cream-colored flower-stalks which emerge from the base of the crownshaft in summer.

Fruit: Pretty, bright red fruit is about 1½ inches long, inedible.

Cultivation: Montgomery palm requires a bright, well-drained location which is free from frost. Water it regularly until it is well established. Fertilize it three times a year and water it in times of drought. It is somewhat tolerant of salt.

In the photo below, the difference in appearance between W. robusta and W. filifera *is clear. The latter species is actually the more "robust"; shorter and stouter, it is also more tolerant of freezing weather.*

Pictured above is W. robusta. *In the photo at left,* W. robusta *is the palm on the left,* W. filifera *is on the right.*

Washington Palm

Because it is fast-growing and virtually care-free, Washington palms are among the most commonly seen palms along the Gulf Coast, as well as in the American Southwest and coastal California, their native range. They eventually attain great heights, often towering over surrounding buildings and other trees.

Also known as: Petticoat palm, desert fan palm, California fan palm, Mexican fan palm, cotton palm, skyduster.

Scientific name: *Washingtonia* spp., named for George Washington.

Native to: Southern California and western Arizona *(W. filifera)*, northwestern Mexico *(W. robusta)*.

Look for: Large, stiff, bright green, fan-shaped leaves; shaggy "skirt" of dead leaves clinging beneath the crown; reddish-brown trunk, sometimes with criss-cross pattern of old leaf bases. *W. filifera* grows to about 50 feet, while *W. robusta* grows as tall as 100 feet.

Blossom: Small, white flowers grow on a stalk which emerges from among the lower leaves; flowers have both male and female parts and appear in spring.

Fruit: Small, dark, oval-shaped fruits are inedible.

Cultivation: Introduced as landscape plants in the southeastern U.S., Washington palms are drought tolerant desert palms. However, this also means they may not grow well in low, wet areas or during periods of excessive rainfall. Although cold hardy, moderately salt tolerant and easy to grow, they may succumb to very severe winter weather. They may be propagated from seed. Its great height makes *W. robusta* vulnerable to lightning strikes.

The foxtail palm is so called because of the appearance of its fronds. Leaflets are arranged circularly around the midrib, giving the leaves a very full, bushy look. The leaflets nearest the trunk may grow very long, reaching almost to the ground.

Foxtail Palm

This attractive palm has become a popular specimen planting only relatively recently. It is fast-growing, has relatively few problems, and is tolerant of a wide range of soil conditions. However, it is not tolerant of cold weather, so it is only appropriate for frost-free locations.

Scientific name: *Wodyetia bifurcata*, after Wodyeti, the aboriginal Australian who introduced the palm to the world in 1978. *"Bifurcata"* refers to this palm's interesting compound leaves.

Native to: Northern Australia.

Look for: Slender, single, gray trunk, ringed with scars from shed leaves. Trunk swollen at base, topped with green crownshaft. Leaves are 8–10 feet in length and have a distinctive bushy appearance, with leaflets that are dark green above and silvery below.

Blossom: Small white flowers appear in spring, both male and female flowers borne on a leafstalk which emerges from below the crownshaft.

Fruit: Reddish-orange, oblong fruit is 2" long, inedible.

Cultivation: Foxtail palm tolerates some salt and drought and is not fussy as to soil type. It is more cold hardy than many tropical palms, but should not be planted in areas that are subject to hard freezes. It does best in full sun with regular fertilization. It may be propagated by seed, which takes several months to germinate.

Bibliography

Bailey, L. H. *Manual of Cultivated Plants*. New York: Macmillan, 1951.

Broschat, Timothy K., and Meerow, Alan W. *Betrock's Reference Guide to Florida Landscape Plants*. Cooper City, FL: Betrock Information Systems, 2001.

Ellison, Don and Anthony Ellison. *Betrock's Cultivated Palms of the World*. Hollywood, FL: Betrock Information Systems, 2001.

Langlois, Arthur C. *Supplement to Palms of the World*. Gainesville, FL: University Presses of Florida, 1976.

Long, Robert W. and Lakela, Olga. *A Flora of Tropical Florida: A Manual of the Seed Plants and Ferns of Southern Peninsular Florida*. Coral Gables, FL: University of Miami Press, 1971.

MacCubbin, Tom. *Florida Home Grown: Landscaping*. Orlando, FL: Sentinel Communications Co., 1987.

McCurrach, James C., *Palms of the World*. New York: Harper & Brothers, 1960 (reprinted in 1970 by Horticultural Books, Stuart, FL).

McGeachy, Beth. *Handbook of Florida Palms*. St. Petersburg, FL: Great Outdoors, 1955.

Meerow, Alan W. *Betrock's Guide to Landscape Palms*. Cooper City, FL: Betrock Information Systems, 2002.

Stresau, Frederic B. *Florida, My Eden*. Port Salerno, FL: Florida Classics Library, 1986.

Watkins, John V., and Sheehan, Thomas J. *Florida Landscape Plants: Native and Exotic* (Revised Edition). Gainesville, FL: University Presses of Florida, 1975.

Wunderlin, Richard P. *Guide to the Vascular Plants of Florida*. Gainesville, FL: University Press of Florida, 1998.

Photo Acknowledgments

A colorful sign tops a gazebo marking the entrance to the Florida Botanical Gardens palm collection, where Florida native and exotic palms are arranged around a fountain in an attractive outdoor setting.

Thanks are owed to the following arboreta, which allowed photos of their specimens to be used in this book. Palm enthusiasts are encouraged to visit them and to support them in their endeavors.

Fairchild Tropical Garden, 10901 Old Cutler Road, Miami, FL 33156, phone (305)667-1651, www.ftg.org.

Florida Botanical Gardens, 12175 125th Street North, Largo, FL 33774, phone (727)582-2100, coop.co.pinellas.fl.us/fbgardens.

Gizella Kopsick Palm Arboretum, 10th Avenue NE and North Shore Drive, St. Petersburg, FL, phone (727)893-7335, www.stpete.org/palm.html.

Marie Selby Botanical Gardens, 811 South Palm Avenue, Sarasota, FL 34236, phone (941)366-5731, www.selby.org.

Mounts Botanical Gardens, 531 Military Trail, West Palm Beach, FL, 33415, phone (561)233-1760, www.mounts.org.

Sarasota Jungle Gardens, 3701 Bayshore Road, Sarasota, FL, 34234, phone (941)355-5305, www.sarasotajunglegardens.com.

University of South Florida Botanical Gardens, 4202 Fowler Avenue, SCA238, Tampa, FL, 33620, phone (813)974-2329, www.cas.usf.edu/garden.

The **International Palm Society** is an international clearinghouse for information about palms. Contact them to learn about their activities and how to join. They may be reached on the world wide web at www.palms.org, or by mail at P.O. Box 7075, Lawrence, KS 66044.

Index